P9-ELT-358

Networks that *Work*

A Practitioner's Guide to Managing Networked Action

Paul Vandeventer

Co-Author/Network Management Advisor and Practitioner

Myrna Mandell, Ph.D.

Co-Author/Network Management Advisor and Researcher

Hershey|Cause, Editing, Production, Promotion

Corky Retson, Design

This book was made possible through the support
of The California Endowment.

Copyright © 2007 by Community Partners. All rights reserved.
No part of this book may be reproduced in any form without
express written permission from the publisher.

Library of Congress Number 2001012345
ISBN 978-0-9763027-3-5

THIS BOOK would not have been possible without the support, contributions and inspiration of the host of network managers, members, funders, practitioners, problem solvers and thinkers working worldwide to solve problems through networked action. Too often these good people find themselves outside the defined boundaries – and attendant comforts – of a professional "field" from which they might draw support and understanding. May this book in some small way help them feel connected to a profoundly skilled and resourceful group of colleagues, to a rich reservoir of scholarly and practical knowledge, and to powers they may not have recognized they possessed.

David Booher provided very early inspiration with his explanations of the ubiquity of conflict in networks and the need for robust conflict management processes as part of any network effort. I feel particularly indebted to Dutch researcher **Dr. Erik-Hans Klijn,** editor with Walter J.M. Kickert and Joop F.M. Koppenjan, of the priceless book *Managing Complex Networks: Strategies* *for the Public Sector*. Dr. Klijn responded with kindness and encouragement to an email I sent him in 2005 proposing a practical guide for network practitioners. From the far reaches of the Netherlands he directed me to my very own Southern California backyard. There I found **Myrna Mandell,** a perceptive and spirited adventurer and researcher, at California State University, Northridge, near Los Angeles. Myrna agreed to conduct the case study interviews, inform the thinking, respond to drafts and bind herself to this project as an intellectual partner.

Much appreciation goes to **The California Endowment,** with special thanks to **Paul Hernandez, Amanda Rounsaville,** and **Dr. Robert Ross** whose excitement and encouragement proved infectious.

Many thanks to the people who thoughtfully reviewed the content, provided their thoughts or added their expertise: **Carlos Alvarado, Anne Duncan, Linda Fowells, Cynthia Freeman, Anna Henderson, Eve Hill, Chuck Hirt, Laura Hogan, Anna Karailieva, Dylan Kendall, Lyndee Knox, Igor Kokarev, Mara Manus, Katherine McFate, Eric Medina, Ellen Sanchez, Yolanda Vera, Gwen Walden, Belinda Walker, Billie Weiss, Eugene Wilson.**

Special thanks to **Corky Retson,** designer, and the production team at Hershey|Cause: editor **Kirsty Burkhart,** proofreader **Patty Park,** and team leader **R. Christine Hershey.**

And our greatest gratitude goes to the network members who shared their experiences for the case studies:

NAAFE: Joe Berry, Jeremy Brecher, Tim Costello, Marcus Courtney, Kim Foltz, Suren Moodliar, Cathy Ruckleshaus

The California Partnership: Nancy Berlin, Mary Ignatius, Alicia Lepe, Joseph Villela

The Water Forum: Jeff Loux, Jonas Minton, Walt Pettit, Susan Sherry, Leo Winternitz

Paul Vandeventer
September 2007

Why *Networks That Work* Now?

As investors like Bill Gates and Warren Buffett pool resources to tackle global issues on an enormous scale, others are realizing the need for similar collective action commensurate with the scale of their missions. In the simplest terms, a "network" refers to any sustained effort around which different, autonomous organizations work in concert as equal partners in pursuit of a common social or civic purpose. Historically independent organizations, agencies and institutions are now more likely to form networks to tackle environmental, health care, childhood, aging and any number of other crises. Their leaders are recognizing the need to leverage trusted relationships with other organizations to extend limited resources and amplify on-the-ground results.

And these joint efforts are expanding beyond any particular sector. Nonprofits are working with businesses, philanthropies with governmental agencies, and loose-knit activist and community groups with well-established institutions.

Unfortunately, coming together doesn't always mean working together. Some networks frankly don't work. In fact, a network can be a double-edged sword. Whether the result of faulty motivation – to meet a funder's requirement, for example – or the inability to overcome past histories, failed networks can squander resources, including trust, time and momentum.

…leaders are recognizing the need to leverage trusted relation-ships with other organizations…

But honest self-assessment, careful planning, clear under-standings and conflict resolution and management can help avoid and overcome obstacles. The three case studies abbreviated in the appendix and fully fleshed out at *www.CommunityPartners.org* provide excellent examples of how a few groups created networks that really work and the success they can achieve.

The Genesis of *Networks That Work*

This guide is a compilation of years of observation and experience. As do many helpful tools, this one emerged from frustration and perplexity. At Community Partners, where scores of civic initiatives incubate and receive fiscal sponsorship under our umbrella, we repeatedly saw alliances and coalitions of nonprofit groups form, struggle and, too often, fail.

Digging deeper for causes, we realized many under-taking these ventures defaulted to classical organizational planning and management approaches that simply did not work when large groups of autonomous organiza-tions with strong-willed leaders sought to work together.

Networks, we discovered, seemed to do better when tended by the deft and gentle hand of a facilitator, rather than the executive hand of a director.

For successful networks, negotiating trade-offs in organizational interests was more the norm than was the necessary fretting common to organizational boards and staffs over mission and vision statements, goals, objectives and action plans. Conflict, we realized, was never far from the surface in most networks, but groups that deliberately expected and planned for the management of conflict functioned effectively, even as they worked through the difficulties of moving from self-interest to common purpose.

We saw the degree to which pre-existing relationships among network members mattered fundamentally to network success. And we realized that the genuine interdependence that is the mark of a collaborative network rarely resulted without members risking loss of turf, power, prestige, even money or a long-prized place in a system that needed changing.

We saw a growing need to share these lessons with any and all considering or navigating a network venture.

How to Use This Guide

If your organization has joined or is considering a networked effort with other groups, if the scale of your mission seems too daunting, too important to tackle alone, if you're looking to leverage your resources and amplify your organizational power, this book is for you. It covers a range of issues to consider before you decide to network, as you create a network and while you pursue networked action – all designed to help your network work.

This book is not, nor could it be, a complete guide to your network, but it does provide tools you'll need to evaluate your options. Also included are rich case studies that bring those options to life, checklists and essential questions to inform your choices, samples of critical materials you're free to use, web links to full case studies of other networks, and a list of other available resources.

It is our hope that this booklet will serve as a helpful resource, one that you will continue to use as you consider, form and evolve your network.

And please, let us know your thoughts. Your feedback will help ensure that any future editions continue to reflect the most current needs and best practices of the full range of networks. Please forward your comments to *networks@CommunityPartners.org*.

CHAPTER 1

What Are Networks?

THE TERM "network" as used in this book refers to many different organizations working in concert as equal partners pursuing a common social or civic purpose over a sustained period of time.

Organizations of all kinds commonly act alone to fulfill civic, community or public interest missions. Sometimes, they discover compelling reasons to join forces, even across different sectors – nonprofit, commercial and governmental – of the civic arena. The goal is to achieve greater social, economic or political impact than is possible alone. These joint efforts – called networks – have many different purposes and operate throughout society.

Some networks, like those formed among nonprofits advocating for social change, simply seek to share information with one another and their memberships. Other networks seek to build power through their collective size and strength to push for legislative, major systems and public policy changes. Still others

A Working Definition

WHAT: Many different organizations working in concert.

WHO: Organizations, institutions, governmental agencies, corporations foundations, etc. (Use of "organizations" in this book, refers to all types of potential network members.)

WHY: Around a common, defined purpose.

HOW: As equal partners.

come together determined to fundamentally alter entrenched, unwieldy, outmoded or unworkable public systems. Networks can bring greater scale and focus, more productive kinds of working relationships and greater, more lasting effectiveness to addressing public problems.

Sometimes referred to as "collaboratives" and "coalitions," networks come together when the scale and complexity of a societal problem exceed any single organization's capacity to tackle it alone. Savvy, practical leaders recognize that many organizations collaborating to address a large problem may also make independent work easier.

To set a course for this collaboration, first acknowledge the distinguishing features of a true network and adopt a form suited to your risk comfort.

Distinctive Features of Networks

Three critical features distinguish networks from the individual organizations and institutions that comprise them:

1. Networks require members to invest in and build new types of relationships and, in varying ways and to differing degrees, acknowledge their mutual interdependence.
2. Networks differ in their level of complexity and, therefore, in the risks they demand of members.
3. No one is "in charge" in a network.

> Networks can bring greater scale and focus, more productive kinds of working relationships and greater, more lasting effectiveness to addressing public problems.

Networks Require New Relationships

The desire to address urgent public problems and important tasks brings network members together. Achieving durable results from working jointly, however, often hinges on how well members relate to one another. Respectful, open working relationships are a prerequisite for successful outcomes:

- Network members must recognize, be prepared to reveal and, sometimes, negotiate their own organizational and institutional interests.
- They must appreciate and respect the interests of other groups, even if that means revising or changing long-held views.
- They must mutually acknowledge that solving a large societal problem depends on their combined efforts and lasting commitment to addressing the problem together.

Increasing Complexity Means Different Levels of Risk

Existing research identifies at least three progressively more complex types of networks, each with higher "stakes" or risks for members. Knowing at the outset what risks you can tolerate will help you decide what kind of network you want to form. Organizing one kind of network may lead to a greater tolerance for risk among the groups and the ability to reorganize in new ways with higher stakes.

No One's "In Charge" In A Network

Relationships in networks rest on a principle of equal partnership, which requires special structural and managerial arrangements. Networks and their member organizations have some significant differences. Executives and managers of independent organizations exercise authority. They are "in charge" – they set direction, pursue opportunities that fulfill the organization's mission, make decisions, direct employees and allocate resources.

Relationships in networks rest on a principle of equal partnership, which requires special structural and managerial arrangements.

Networks function on the principle of what researchers label "divided" or "shared" authority. No member can tell another member what to do because all members are autonomous and independent organizations. None want to place decisions about what they do in an outsider's hands.

A network manager's job is different from an organization executive's job. Whether they are paid employees functioning in the role of network manager or a group of network members functioning voluntarily as a management committee or steering group, successful network managers generally do not direct. They serve very little as planners, designers and leaders. Rather, they act as process coordinators and facilitators. In general, a network manager's role is to:

- Help members communicate, share information, clarify interests and define genuine differences.
- Help members identify what tasks need to be performed to fulfill the network's purpose.

- Guide, smooth and create efficient interactions as members go about the network's tasks.
- Spot favorable opportunities members can pursue to address and resolve issues that brought the network into existence in the first place.
- Locate and help secure resources.
- Build the network by identifying and helping to bring in new members.
- Seek ways to refresh and renew the network's capabilities and functions.

In short, network managers handle the complexity that naturally arises when large, diverse collections of groups work on any project. They do so constantly mindful that they are in service to the greater good embodied in the network's purpose and in the agreements network members have made in deciding to work together.

Three Different Types of Networks

The different types of networks can be broken down into at least three categories:

Cooperating Networks
Coordinating Networks
Collaborating Networks

Cooperating Networks involve relatively low levels of risk. They lead to little, if any, systemic or large-scale social, economic or political reform. However, in these kinds of networks, members often:

- Create social environments that lead to better personal and professional relationships.
- Experiment with more trust-based forms of engagement.
- Model and explain best practices for one another.
- Share information and work jointly to document problems.
- Test ideas and learn about different approaches to one another's work in committees or work groups.
- Convene problem-solving or issue discussion sessions.

Coordinating Networks involve low to moderate risk to members. In addition to many of the activities that distinguish cooperating networks, groups and organizations in coordinating networks:

- Carefully identify and pursue service or advocacy priorities.
- Negotiate time, resource and energy commitments with other network members.
- Push established organizational boundaries and establish a more robust sense of mutual interdependence.
- Strengthen individual and institutional relationships by engaging in activities that require greater mutual reliance.

Collaborating Networks involve high stakes and, therefore, involve higher degrees of member risk. In addition to many of the activities associated with cooperating and coordinating networks, organizations and institutions involved in collaborating networks:

- Generally have joined together to pursue fundamental, long-term system creation or reform of some kind.
- Have methods in place for surfacing, addressing and resolving conflicts.
- All have representation in the network and must agree upon, work within and self-enforce the tasks required to achieve and maintain the new or reformed system.
- Typically begin to "give up" old notions and begin to think differently about how the system in which they have been working can work differently.
- Authentically participate in or advocate for fundamental resource reallocation in ways that, under the old system, they may have resisted or protected.
- Reach agreement on how to permanently and often radically alter or shift the ways they once operated.
- Reformulate and redefine the ways in which they play their various roles within a larger system.

Across the network spectrum, success depends on members participating with their eyes wide open and without illusions, delusions or posturing about what they hope to accomplish by working together.

Potential risks for members of a network increase in correlation to the scale of the desired change. At the outset, groups affiliating as networks need to gauge their own comfort with and commitment to change. They need to assess the degree to which they are prepared to invest in creating changes that – in the name of improved public value – may alter policies, systems and resource streams upon which they have grown reliant.

...success depends on members participating with their eyes wide open...

For many groups the risks, constraints, exposure and demands of network participation may be uncomfortable, even unbearable. In such cases, groups always have the choice of operating independently. If an organization or institution, however, chooses to operate in a network, they always have the choice of creating or participating in one that comes with a greater or lesser degree of risk in accordance with their comfort.

1. **The North American Alliance for Fair Employment (NAAFE)** illustrates the behavior of a cooperating network, perhaps the most common form. In small groups, members did what they thought important; a variety of activities occurred more in pursuit of incremental system changes that members hoped might eventually add up to larger system reforms. As a result, a number of campaigns got information out widely on a variety of issues. The group as a whole valued a high degree of sharing among autonomous and independent organizations and the risks they took tended to cross very little into the organizational boundaries each group considered its own. [page 67]

2. **The California Partnership** illustrates the behavior of a coordinating network. Its members work together as a whole, but each organization still maintains autonomy. The network comes together on issues that affect most of the member organizations and acts as a coordinating mechanism allowing them to get issues on the table or perform tasks that will benefit them individually and collectively. They take more risks, but still maintain their independent status as separate organizations, albeit coordinating their activities. [page 71]

3. **The Water Forum** illustrates the behavior and character of a collaborating network. The organizations in this network, in several instances after decades of litigation and conflict, have come together to work on very complex issues of water resource allocation, regulation and watershed or habitat protection that none could handle or successfully resolve alone. The members spent a lot of time recognizing their essential *inter*dependence and the need to change the ways they conducted business. They concentrated on building new relationships and establishing trust among members who previously only had contentious relationships. Willing to look at their fundamental approach to water issues, the network made major changes across a very complex system of water delivery and watershed management. They have agreed to work together for 30 years and recognize the need to take great risks. [page 75]

Three Types of Networks Illustrated

The three major network types cited in this book are **cooperating, coordinating** and **collaborating** networks. The three case studies in the Appendices cover all three network types.

CHAPTER 2

What to Consider *Before* You Start

WORKING IN NETWORKS CAN PROVE CHALLENGING, even difficult. As noted earlier, not every group has the appetite for the risk, potential conflict or hard work. Too often, groups allow funders and others to push them into working together when they are ill-prepared for the endeavor. Terms like "collaboratives" and "coalitions" get thrown around routinely as if good will and success are just a matter of gathering folks around the same table. Working from the wrong motivations can thwart progress in addressing large societal problems, waste resources, disappoint expectations and even hurt people in vulnerable communities.

But, the right motivations can unleash creative energy, advance needed change and lead to fundamentally reformed social systems and public policies. In addition to examining your motivations, carefully weigh the advantages and disadvantages of networked action before venturing ahead.

With All the Risk and Hard Work, Why Form a Network?

Risks, Pitfalls, Problems, and Solutions

In building a network, organizations may need to tackle a number of challenges head on, particularly past experiences. If left unaddressed, very real and legitimate organizational histories, distinctive preferences for ways of working and attitudes about other groups or about collaboration in general can interfere with consensus building, hinder effectiveness and lead to misunderstanding and wrong assumptions. Bringing in skilled facilitators who have interest-negotiating tools, who can train network members in conflict resolution skills, and who simply understand ways to make meetings work well can help surface and defuse some of these issues which typically include:

- Members tied to unique organizational histories, ideologies or peculiarities.
- Strong or exclusive member claims to particular physical, programmatic, political, operational, demographic and even moral territory or "turf."
- Insistence upon particular approaches to and methods for solving problems.

If the previous points are not addressed at the very beginning, a number of other challenges or problems will arise, including:

- Lost investments of time, energy and resources if different groups cannot agree on a clearly defined joint purpose.

...the right motivations can unleash creative energy, advance needed change and lead to fundamentally reformed social systems and public policies.

- Potentially lethal land mines if groups refuse up front to face conflict-producing issues and whatever relational, competitive or historic tensions that may divide them.
- Conflict, confusion and disagreement over what "problem" the network is trying to solve.
- Misunderstandings and potential offense if members fail to treat one another as entirely equal partners, no matter the social, political or economic strength of individual groups.
- Undue complication of otherwise ordinary issues (communications, management and conflict resolution) that result any time many groups work together.
- Deflated expectations – and possible reluctance to work together in the future – if groups aspire to an ambitious purpose and then neglect to find or dedicate the human, financial and other resources to its fulfillment.
- Individual feelings of disempowerment, betrayal, burnout, fatigue and hopelessness resulting from poor management.

Still, these hurdles can be overcome in a variety of ways if network members consciously:

- Make sure everyone understands from the outset that the process can take a long time – sometimes even years – and work to achieve small yet essential "wins" in the short term as the network develops.
- Emphasize reframing problems or issues, not based on members' individual perspectives, but rather on a new perspective rooted in the key areas of agreement among all members.

- Recognize from the beginning this is a new type of process and a new way of working. Understand participants may require training in how to deal with each other in new ways and may need experts or outside counsel with specialized skills.
- Make sure all participants have the approval of the key decision makers in their parent organizations and have the full authority to make decisions before starting the network.
- Insist all participants routinely advise their parent organizations of the progress and the difficulties throughout the process.
- Make certain the key decision makers – not the day-to-day representatives – from the parent organizations commit their organizations by signing any network agreements.

After carefully considering the potential challenges and various means of addressing them, weigh the advantages of networks – to both individual organizations and to the larger societal purpose at the network's core.

Some Advantages of Networks

Despite – and sometimes as a direct result of – the challenges of forming a network, networks can and do work on multiple levels. They can help focus both independent and collective efforts, expand best practices and amplify results. Indeed, organizations working together in networks can open themselves to a variety of distinct advantages, including:

- More effectively delivered services that meaningfully address human needs, improve civic life and enable people to determine their own destiny and that of their community.
- Greater influence and power through larger numbers and sharper focus.
- Greater impact through aligned activities.
- Robust written agreements that form the basis for sustained commitment to genuine interdependence and lead to wider, more lasting changes.
- Strengthened, more trusting personal and professional relationships achieved through greater openness and shared struggle toward solving public problems.
- Greater knowledge of others' approaches and methods.

Given both the potential risks and advantages, no group should enter lightly into creating or participating in a network. Know what to look for, how to assess your own internal tolerances for risk and what to expect of yourself and others before committing to network involvement.

Checklist: Four Key Questions

When weighing the pros and cons of forming a network, consider at least four questions, including:

1. Do we really want to do this?
2. What do we hope to accomplish?
3. Who do we need to have on board?
4. How will we fund the network's activities?

The checklists beneath each question will help leaders assess whether network participation is right for their organizations.

1. **Do we really want to do this?**

Forming networks involves new risks and inevitable difficulties: long-range time and resource commitment, vulnerability to outside scrutiny, greater potential accountability to others, tolerance for operational differences and the possibility of lasting change.

- CAN WE COMMIT SUFFICIENT TIME AND RESOURCES? Networks require long-term member investments of money, staff time, material and intellectual energy, always with the expectation that such jointly committed resources will advance each group's independent mission. The return on such investments will likely accumulate over time rather than be immediately apparent. Temper expectations of immediate results and plan for long-term commitment.

- ARE WE READY FOR INTENSE SCRUTINY? Sustained time across the table from other groups invariably opens up any organization's values, interests and effectiveness to critical examination. To prepare, conduct a searching internal organizational self-assessment.

- ARE WE PREPARED TO HOLD OURSELVES ACCOUNTABLE TO AGREEMENTS? Effective networks require clarity about joint purpose and agreement about priority action areas and necessary follow-through. Agreements carry with them the implicit expectation that members will seriously strive to achieve results.

- CAN WE TOLERATE DIFFERENCES WITH THE WAY OTHER GROUPS WORK? Unique organizational cultures and histories mean that no two organizations will ever likely share the same exact definition of the societal problem they want to solve or the goals they will pursue in solving it. A network's advantage is that groups maintain their autonomy and can march to their own beat even while they align their efforts with other groups. Yet, networks can falter if they lack methods of dealing with members that block progress, whose representatives don't participate or whose behavior proves disruptive or destructive. For best results, approach network participation expecting wide variation in perspectives and differences in problem solving approaches.

> A network's advantage is that groups maintain their autonomy and can march to their own beat even while they align their efforts with other groups.

- HOW PREPARED ARE WE TO PURSUE AUTHENTIC CHANGE? Forming or joining a network can lead to or stem from the recognition that the status quo no longer works – in a service delivery system, in a set of public policies or among agency leaders who do not know one another or work together. To varying degrees, networks demand or result in real and lasting change in systems, institutional relationships, policies, programs and funding streams. Enter networks assuming that change will occur and understand your tolerance for or resistance to the consequences.

2. What do we hope to accomplish?

Define the core purpose that will bind the network together. Even if it evolves over time, the motivating purpose, captured in writing, represents the clearest statement about what the network wants to accomplish. Clarity of purpose also helps shape understanding of the kind of network under construction and the associated risks.

- DO WE EMBRACE THE NETWORK'S PURPOSE? To streamline information sharing, a cooperating network with relatively low levels of risk and resource demands may be optimal. Activities may include a Web site with chat or blog capabilities, regular print or online newsletters, sharing of in-depth case studies, news reports and scholarly research disseminated among network members and periodic gatherings combining learning and social interaction opportunities. For ambitions of achieving larger-scale change, defining the common purpose may require more time, introspection on core organizational self-interests and finding ways to surface and resolve any differences with other groups. Given the higher risks and greater resource commitments of coordinating and collaborating networks, consider and adopt reliable methods for resolving disputes likely to arise in the course of the network's life.

- CAN THE NETWORK'S PURPOSE ALSO ADVANCE OUR ORGANIZATIONAL OR INSTITUTIONAL MISSION? Organizational self-interest must be a component of network participation – though not the exclusive or even primary driver. The broader network purpose should energize the individual work, even though rooted in self-interest, of member organizations. Otherwise, something is amiss and requires deeper exploration. However, network members must expect to seriously negotiate interests, trade-offs and risks in service to the common purpose – the shared interests – that bind the network together.

- ARE STRONG MECHANISMS IN PLACE TO WORK STEADILY TOWARD ACHIEVING THE NETWORK PURPOSE? Clear articulation of purpose and the development of working relationships and processes can be frustrating. Even when personal and organizational relationships have strong, deep roots, some communal "storming" must occur before the group figures out the best path with the fewest obstacles. Groups need clarity about themselves and the history of the problem they are uniting to address as they make choices about what activities and structures will support their efforts. Some may need outside consultants with the skills, competency and objectivity needed to facilitate working relationships among network members. Skilled facilitators or even mediators can help the group get over tough spots and train network members in conflict-resolution and interest-negotiation techniques. Networks may also require staff with a variety of network management, technology, resource development and financial or administrative skills.

> Groups need clarity about themselves and the history of the problem they are uniting to address...

3. Who do we need to have on board?

When evaluating a potential network, take into account the players who need to be at the table and invest in the network's purpose, as well as those who need to support the network in other ways.

- WHAT'S THE RIGHT SIZE AND COMPOSITION OF THE NETWORK'S MEMBERSHIP? The choice and number of network participants should bear a strong correlation to the scale and history of the societal problem the network seeks to resolve. Depending on the problem, the network may require participants from different sectors— commercial, civic, nonprofit, governmental or labor.

The choice and number of network participants should bear a strong correlation to the scale and history of the societal problem the network seeks to resolve.

- DO ALL MEMBERS NEED TO SHARE THE SAME POINT OF VIEW? Take into account participation by groups with different or even conflicting definitions of the problem. They may be essential to addressing the problem. Consciously and carefully approach any decisions to ignore or exclude organized interest groups operating outside, and potentially at cross-purposes with, the network. These decisions are important because the ignored or excluded will very likely affect priorities as the network progresses.

- DOES EVERY GROUP NEED TO HAVE THE SAME LEVEL OF COMMITMENT TO THE NETWORK? Some networks may define varying levels of participation for different organizations or groups. For example, individuals not affiliated with organizations may still bring value to the network and be welcomed but with modified resource

commitment expectations. Some networks grant
"observer" status to representatives who are not direct
network members, but who can learn from or bring value
to the network's deliberative process. Even while thinking
about participants, consider the range of outside support
the network will need to succeed. Subject matter experts
or academics may provide critical information, perspective and analysis.

- DOES OUR NETWORK NEED OTHER KINDS OF SUPPORT-
ERS? Equally as important, and perhaps supremely so,
make sure that influential people – think: "movers and
shakers" – in the community or within the arena of the
network's purpose support the network. These "sponsors"
can provide critical "civic sanction" to network activities.
Sponsors may include past or present legislators or other
public officials, respected leaders of funding organizations, past or present university presidents, legal system
luminaries, and other people of indisputable civic stature.
Although not necessarily members of the network, sponsors lend their prestige and blessing to the network and
ensure its legitimacy, elevate its activities and accomplishments, and confer tacit approval – even protection from
assaults on credibility – that can make a difference to
continued network operation.

4. How will we fund the network's activities?

Network operational expenses can vary greatly depending
on what members intend to accomplish and their expectations of network activities.

- HOW EXPENSIVE IS PARTICIPATING IN THE NETWORK GOING TO BE? To the degree that some level of expense will accompany the network's operation, expect to participate in footing the costs or securing outside resources. Simply stated, funding and resource commitment demands come with the territory. The more challenging the territory, the greater the need will be for funds to sustain the network. That said, money and other resources should ease, not impede network effectiveness. Networks have found surprisingly creative ways to meet the necessary resource commitments, some of which will receive greater attention later on in this booklet.

- WHAT ASSETS SHOULD WE PREPARE TO BRING TO THE TABLE? Recognize from the outset that any network's greatest assets lie in the mission focus, leadership strength, program vigor, fiscal and administrative stability and funding relationships that already exist within member organizations. Strong, stable and reasonably well-funded network members can enhance and even accelerate a network's effectiveness. Financially weak and otherwise anemic members should not assume they will somehow reap financial windfalls from network participation.
In anticipating network resource demands, determine which network functions require cash and which can be supplied in-kind by members.

- SHOULD WE EXPECT TO GAIN FINANCIALLY BY PARTICIPATING IN A NETWORK? Groups need to have the fiscal vision and confidence, coupled with the steadiness of commitment, to see that network success will likely feed long-term organizational success in addressing critical social, system and policy problems. Achieving large gains in those arenas generally makes for a good investment of organizational assets. Still, the hope of gaining immediate fiscal advantage is the least constructive of all initial reasons for joining a network. More than one network has formed around the availability of money and fallen apart as soon as that money stream dried up.

- **WHAT OTHER CONSIDERATIONS ABOUT MONEY SHOULD WE THINK ABOUT IN ADVANCE?** Consider and appreciate that there are certain stability advantages that come with sustained and reliable funding streams. There are also trade-offs depending on the source of funds. Foundation and other outside, non-network members may want to impose expectations or controls. The relationship between who funds the network and any expectations of control attached to funding need to be thought through carefully.

After weighing all the considerations, if you decide to organize a network, you will need to address many specific topics and logistics. Turn to the next chapter for 13 essential questions that will help you as you move ahead with your network.

CHAPTER 3

What to Consider As You Create a Network

THE QUESTIONS DISCUSSED on the following pages have an obvious logic to their sequence; you will invariably find yourself considering aspects of all the questions simultaneously as formative deliberations proceed. Keep a record of issues raised and decisions made around each question during this process to facilitate the drafting of a network agreement (sometimes called a memorandum of understanding, a network charter, or a relational contract; see *Sample Template for a Network Agreement* provided as Appendix E in this booklet) when the time comes to do so. Essential questions to address include:

- What purpose drives our network?
- What determines network participation and defines who should join the network?
- How firm is member commitment to this network?
- To what extent does the network have continuous outside support or sponsorship?
- How will we organize, manage and govern the network?
- How do we determine and organize our action priorities?
- What methods will we use to establish new relationships?

Thirteen Essential Questions

- How will we conduct our work?
- What kind of agreement should we make to function as a network?
- How do network members hold themselves and one another accountable?
- How will we resolve conflicts?
- What funding and other resources will fuel the network?
- What other key resources do we need to have in place?

1. **What purpose drives our network?**

...focus on crafting a clear, specific and unambiguous statement of the network's purpose.

Shared purpose drives all networks. Take care not to confuse purpose and problem. Defining the network's shared purpose differs from reaching universal agreement on the social, civic or public interest problem as each member organization may define it. Because every member brings a different history, perspective and organizational mission to the network, any hope of universal agreement on the problem may remain elusive. Instead, focus on crafting a clear, specific and unambiguous statement of the network's purpose.

For example, The Water Forum, one of the groups profiled in this booklet on page 75 expressed its two-prong purpose as follows:

- Provide a reliable and safe water supply for the Sacramento region's economic health and planned development to the year 2030; and,
- Preserve the fishery, wildlife, recreational, and aesthetic values of the Lower American River.

2. What determines participation and defines who should join the network?

Networks that work consist of people representing organizations and institutions who share some degree of pre-existing relationship with one another. The character of pre-existing relationships may range across a wide spectrum, from loose familiarity with one another's work to a shared and contentious history, with many variations in between. Networks form principally because members want – and often need – new kinds of relationships that will help them fulfill organizational, institutional and greater public missions.

The formative stage of a network involves a peculiar sorting process as groups consider the problem that needs solving and the stakes they are willing to risk in partnering with others to solve it. This process leads to networks with the varying characteristics identified earlier as cooperative, coordinative and collaborative. Groups may find themselves considering and reconsidering the stakes and associated risks as new kinds of relationships evolve. Network members need to know how to talk about the stakes and risks candidly. They also need to know, in scoping out the problem, their tolerance for opening network membership to other groups essential to the effort. Will the network accept new members? Under what circumstances and what terms? Groups will come into networks, it is fair to say, for a variety of reasons and they may choose to stay for new reasons they can only discover once they have accepted the commitments expected of participants.

3. How firm is member commitment to this network?

Once networks organize around and define the terms of engagement and a clear purpose, commitment to the network must remain strong or the network risks weakness and drift. Often networks specify that member organizations must designate representatives to the network. The weight of each representative's decision-making authority in his or her organization is indicative of the organization's larger commitment to the network purpose. In making agreements, deliberating issues, negotiating interests, confirming information or taking action, a representative's need to consult or confer with the member organization will speed up or slow down the network's progress. A representative's authority should be commensurate with the issues the network is addressing; the higher the stakes, the higher the representative's authority needs be. One rule of thumb: Any network agreement carries only as much authority and weight as the people who make and sign the agreement carry in their own organizations or institutions.

4. To what extent does the network have continuous outside support or sponsorship?

When previously unaffiliated groups make the decision to organize as a network, it speaks volumes about each group's determination to address a public problem in new ways. Still, outside political, civic or institutional support – sometimes called "sponsorship" – can make a decisive difference in network effectiveness. Sometimes that sponsorship may come from local elected leaders or prestigious individuals with broad civic, governmental, labor or business sector stature. Carefully assess and enlist outside support with sufficient clout to make sure the network has, from the start, the greatest promise for sustainability.

5. **How do we determine and organize our action priorities?**

Determining priorities begins even as representatives move toward clarity about the network purpose. Members rank action priorities around their relative urgency, importance and estimated timeframe needed for resolution. Priorities should emerge from a measured, respectful exploration of member interests with the shared aim being the best possible alignment of interests. The process must allow both time and safe space in which members can voice and clarify what each finds essential to achieving the network's purpose from the vantage point of their particular mission.

Because groups assemble and establish networks in response to large-scale public problems, representatives need to realize that fluid factors in the external environment require networks to remain nimble in reorganizing priorities if changing conditions warrant. Sudden or even gradual shifts in the political, social or economic environment require agility and responsiveness on the part of network members. Network representatives must keep abreast of evolving conditions and build space in the network to share perspectives and evaluate the impact of change.

Carefully assess and enlist outside support with sufficient clout to make sure the network has, from the start, the greatest promise for sustainability.

Network priorities often become the focus of work groups (discussed below), active subsets of network members who maintain an open line of communication back to the entire network.

6. How will we organize, manage and govern the network?

Networks operate not on the basis of single-authority hierarchies (as do most individual organizations) and member rank, but rather on the basis of equal partnership and divided-authority structures. Equal partnership and divided-authority require profound mutual respect for the autonomy, interests, voice and effectiveness of each organization or institution committed to the network and its purpose. Nevertheless, members in all vital, active networks very likely will seek to influence one another in various ways. Networks have distinct political features with complex inter-organizational dynamics, deeply valued interests, a mixture of highly motivated personalities and members with constituencies that need satisfying. Successful network politics is more likely to come from members working to persuade one another based on the merits of shared interests rather than on their dominating size, economic clout, political muscle, social or civic status and other distinctions.

Network members can model themselves upon a variety of organizing structures or create hybrid forms of their own. Possibilities include:

SELF-GOVERNING GENERAL ASSEMBLY WITH TEAM STRUCTURES. Members function by making purpose and priority decisions as a general assembly; teams in the form of "work groups" or "action groups" take on tasks and activities related to advancing network priorities; and members select and hold accountable a small coordinating group responsible for administrative matters such as developing budgets, managing finances and serving as a reporting group for employees or contractors. This structure may require the convenience and advantages that come with the legal form of a tax-exempt, public benefit corporation. Alternatively, the capacities and potentially valuable neutrality of a tax-exempt fiscal sponsoring organization may be of greatest benefit. Examples include: Community Partners in Los Angeles, Tides Center in San Francisco, Colorado Nonprofit Development Center in Denver, or Third Sector New England in Boston.

LEAD ORGANIZATION STRUCTURE. In this approach, one member organization or institution is nominally "in charge" but the overriding terms of equal partnership apply. The lead organization cannot direct – nor be perceived as seeking to direct – the decisions, priorities or activities of the network in any way. Instead, the lead organization takes responsibility – perhaps as all or part of its in-kind resource commitment to the network – for certain operational, financial and administrative aspects of the network, effectively extending sponsorship while trusting the network to control its own agenda and activities. Network members may enter into a separate side agreement with the lead organization detailing the terms of the lead organization's role, responsibilities and resource commitment. Alternatively, members can incorporate details of the lead organization's roles, responsibilities and boundaries directly into the written network agreement (discussed in greater detail later).

NETWORK MANAGER STRUCTURE. Able to integrate quite neatly with either or both of the previous two approaches, the network selects someone to function as the network manager. This role may also be referred to as an administrator, coordinator or facilitator. The term "director," which works well in single-authority structures, works poorly for this role. Because of the position's pivotal importance, choosing the network manager requires full agreement from all network members. The roles played by network managers differ significantly from those played by the executive directors and line managers of individual organizations. Network managers understand and navigate the complex relationships among members, always seeking to recognize and help members capitalize on opportunities, clarify member interests, identify conflicts, facilitate communication, maximize available resources, mediate differences and influence the network's capacity to fulfill its purpose. Good network managers are masters at handling strategic complexity with cool and calm, using tools that anticipate and resolve conflict, and always keeping their ego in the right place.

Good network managers are masters at handling strategic complexity with cool and calm...

Network governance becomes the collective obligation of all network members working together around agreements about how they will behave toward and with one another in fulfilling a shared purpose. No separate and distant board of directors sets policy, approves plans and sits back waiting for others to implement them. Members decide priorities and member organizations, in concert, act upon those decisions.

7. **What methods will we use to establish new relationships?**

Recognizing the importance of forming new relationships to advance organizational or institutional work or change systems often motivates the creation of networks or follows quickly on the heels of organizing one. To form new relationships, members need a variety of formal and informal processes to strengthen and deepen the essential bonds of trust and confidence necessary for network success. Too easily dismissed as "touchy-feely," relationship work – as this booklet and the experience of network participants routinely show – lies at the core of effective networks.

Some useful informal relationship-building methods that can impact members' perceptions about one another include shared meals, organized social events, team- and trust-building retreats (such as ropes courses), and other activities that focus less on the network's business and member interests and more on helping member representatives set power differences aside and see one another as individual human beings. Site visits to other members' workplaces can further enhance members' perceptions of one another. Day-long or extended trips to places of interest that reflect members' common civic or community interests also can offer both formal and informal opportunities for new relationships to develop.

Formal methods that establish and integrate rules, roles, responsibilities and routines into the network can range widely. Some examples include:

ESTABLISH EXPECTATIONS FOR STANDARDS OF CONDUCT. Groups work better when, at the outset, members set basic ground rules for expected conduct. Such rules tend to work best when they assume mutual tolerance and include a healthy dose of generosity, particularly when anticipating the inevitable – though often productive – conflicts or debates that attend networked action. Sanctions for violating standards of conduct, however, should be spelled out and upheld by the group.

ADOPT AND USE EFFECTIVE MEETING METHODS. Written material and real-time training abound in how to set up, manage and run effective meetings. *Making Meetings Work* (Doyle and Strauss) is an evergreen source of wisdom, insight and techniques. Since most network activity will revolve around face-to-face interaction in both small and large group meetings, identifying and investing time in learning meeting techniques will pay off in efficiency and results. Any network that hires a manager must include meeting facilitation skills in its job description.

Site visits to other members' workplaces can further enhance members' perceptions of one another.

ADOPT PROVEN DECISION-MAKING TECHNIQUES.
Arriving at agreement can take time. Skilled meeting
facilitators and managers know many techniques for
helping groups consider and make decisions. Simple,
effective techniques, such as those taught by Sam
Kaner, Ph.D., and the trainers from California-based
Community at Work, can help groups in the negotiation process while minimizing frustration and hostility.
Network members generally find "majority rules"
unacceptable for decisions because of the potential for
leaving out the concerns of so many members. Some
networks prefer to operate by allowing negotiated
consensus to develop slowly over time. Some might
seek and act on recommended courses of action from
interest groups, action groups or special task forces
comprised of members.

ADOPT PROVEN CONFLICT RESOLUTION METHODS.
As discussed later in this chapter, groups need to
anticipate and surface conflicts and meet them with
proven methods of conflict management and dispute
resolution. Disputes can arise for many reasons, not
the least of which is member realization that high
stakes may be on the line over scarce resources if
fundamental system change is the network's purpose.
A robust dispute resolution method may assure all
network members they can move through a negotiation process in which all of their respective interests
will be fairly weighed. Training and practice in dispute
resolution techniques can be especially critical in
collaborating networks where stakes and risks are
highest. Success requires agreeing at the outset on

what type of technique to use, training all members in how it works, orienting new network members as they come aboard, and reviewing the results from time to time to assure they still support the network's purpose.

8. How will we conduct our work?

Operational nuts and bolts will evolve over time as the network hones its focus, develops momentum and starts producing results desired by its members. Networks should not struggle to organize activities the way most organizations struggle through strategic planning. The customary struggles with mission statements, by-laws, complicated board governance structures, voting procedures, committee assignments and other such trappings of classically structured organizations will divert precious member attention and energy. Case studies demonstrate newly formed networks can work from a strong unifying purpose and a few simple structures that will foster greater efficiency and facilitate immediate action. A few examples are:

INTEREST GROUPS. Interest groups – subsets of members with similar perspectives – serve as one means for members to organize themselves and conduct work. Open interest group meetings, accessible and transparent to all members, build trust across the network.

WORK GROUPS. Also referred to as task groups or action groups, work groups are another means of developing, refining and addressing network priorities.

A cross-section of the general network membership, they provide a place where members can delve more deeply into issues. Action groups allow members with specific interests in certain network priorities to gather and sustain a dialogue that helps them understand each other and align their work. In addition to fostering trust, open work group meetings break up work into manageable pieces that smaller groups with expertise and knowledge can handle more effectively.

COORDINATING AND ADMINISTRATIVE OVERSIGHT GROUPS. A small coordination group willing to keep the network budget on track, handle finances, execute employment agreements, coordinate reviews of any network staff and generally attend to financial and administrative matters will help keep the network running smoothly. The group derives a certain amount of authority entirely from the consent of all the network members and remains fully accountable to them. This subset or committee should handle money matters with the utmost transparency and discretion. Note that this group has no governance or directive authority over the network or its members. The committee is explicitly not in charge, makes no determination of network priorities, and has no role whatsoever in evaluating or passing judgment on the work of the network in fulfilling its purpose.

NUMBER, FREQUENCY AND KINDS OF MEETINGS. Most networks quickly develop routines around the number, timing and purpose of their meetings. Frequency depends on the kinds and urgency of issues at hand. Regular assemblies of the entire membership produce the greatest results if members meet in between these sessions as part of smaller work groups. Representatives bring updates of working group meetings and any needed requests for general membership decisions to the assembly. General sessions may use a standard agenda of routine items, always leaving room for new issues warranting network attention. Convened as frequently as needed without becoming onerous, general assemblies provide an excellent forum in which to bring forward issues related to the network purpose and likely to influence the network's effectiveness. Between convenings, some work may benefit from periodic conference calls, small group meetings or teleconferences if the technology is available.

9. **What kind of agreement should we make to function as a network?**

Network members generally want the confidence and sense of completion that comes with a written document reflecting their mutual agreements. Variously referred to as memoranda of understanding, compacts, charters, relational contracts or, simply, agreements, these documents reflect the decisions made on the range of matters discussed in the previous section. Depending on the network's purpose, the agreement may address a range of other needs or concerns that arise in the process of establishing the network. Written agreements, whatever the name, serve as a continuous reference point as the network embarks on its activities. They also provide a

way of orienting or presenting the network to other
interested audiences. No single model exists because all
networks are unique. Depending on the type of network,
agreements should address some or all of the following
elements:

- Reasons for Agreement
- Network Purpose
- Network Priorities
- Membership
- Roles, Responsibilities and Commitments of Members
- Operational Structure and Procedures
- Role of Staff and Other Needed Support
- Funding and Resources
- Accountability

The examples discussed in the appendices of this booklet
provide helpful practical examples of networks in action
and links to organizational Web sites, including to some
actual examples of network agreements. The *Sample
Template for a Network Agreement* provided as an
appendix in this booklet explains specific agreement
elements in more depth.

10. **How do network members hold themselves and
one another accountable?**

Because networks are voluntary in nature, their members
voluntarily – rather than legally – enforce network
agreements. The agreements represent a voluntary set
of commitments made by members who can decide at
any time to leave the network and not fulfill future

No single model
exists because
all networks are
unique.

commitments spelled out in the agreement. However, if the agreement is a product of every member's basic interests openly and honestly negotiated, then little reason exists for groups to leave the network. High turnover of members or spotty or low rates of participation should represent a giant red flag that something is amiss. Networks may experience instances in which one or another member or group of members with similar interests feels the "other guys" are not living up to the letter or spirit of the agreement. Approached as an opportunity, these trials can result in continued or voluntarily re-opened interest negotiations, some new understandings among members and modifications of the agreement. Every agreement needs some flexibility since conditions may change, new research or more information may become available and members' organizations may evolve. The more the signatories to the agreement keep each other honest and keep one another talking, the more the agreement becomes self-enforcing and the more likely issues can be resolved with additional negotiation.

High turnover of members or spotty or low rates of participation should represent a giant red flag that something is amiss.

11. How will we resolve conflicts?

Network participants should keep two key points in mind when dealing with conflicts in any type of network. First, conflict comes with the territory and should not be avoided or pushed under the rug. Managing conflict is essential, but conflict properly handled can produce new ideas and synergy upon which to build solutions to problems. Second, the capacity of network participants to deal with conflict depends upon the quality of trust shared among the members. No matter what the issue, network members will find an inescapable correlation between effective conflict resolution and trusting relationships. This makes the need to engage in activities, tasks and behaviors that strengthen and deepen relationships a key feature of successful networks. In addition, especially in collaborating networks, participants must envision, negotiate and build fundamentally new types of relationships that mirror and support the system changes and reforms at the heart of their network's purpose.

Alongside tried and true informal methods for enhancing human relations, like social events and breaking bread together, participants in different networks use varied methods to address and resolve conflict. Here are some examples:

STRUCTURED TRAINING SESSIONS IN INTER-PROFESSIONAL LEADERSHIP through which participants learn new theories, develop a shared language and skills, and, potentially, unlearn old or outmoded behaviors. This method was used by a network called the Service Integration Project, the details of which can be found in an article by Keast, et.al, *Public Administration Review*, May/June 2004, Vol. 64, No. 3, pages 363-371.

STRUCTURED TRAINING SESSIONS on how to negotiate with each other in non-confrontational ways. This method is based on "interest-based negotiations" in which participants surface and discuss their underlying interests, rather than their positions on issues in conflict, as a means of finding and establishing common ground. These methods were used in The Water Forum case, which is summarized in this booklet.

DEVELOPING AND SIGNING FORMAL AGREEMENTS spelling out participants' understanding of their roles and responsibilities in the network. Also referred to as relational contracts and discussed elsewhere in this booklet, more is available on this method in an article by Innes & Booher, "Consensus Building as Role Playing and Bricolage", *Journal of the American Planning Association*, Winter 1999, Vol. 65, No. 1, pages 9-26.

FACILITATED CONSENSUS BUILDING DISCUSSIONS that allow all participants to be heard and encourage respectful and open-ended dialogue. Some methods that have been used to achieve this involve scenario building, storytelling and role playing. Innes & Booher, mentioned above, discuss this in the same article.

INDEPENDENTLY CONDUCTED AND REPORTED FACT-FINDING RESEARCH invited by network members. This compels network members to consider and learn about the larger factual picture surrounding the systems in which they operate and around issues in conflict. From this, presumably, they can achieve a better understanding upon which to frame views and seek network-based solutions.

GATHERING STAFF FROM DIFFERENT NETWORK MEMBER ORGANIZATIONS and co-locating in offices or other settings either permanently or temporarily. Here, network members can more easily learn from one another and use this knowledge to advise their respective organizations. Co-located staff facilitates better communication among network participants, potentially defusing conflicts before they arise. The location may be within a member organization's existing space and dedicated to the network or it may be a new site.

In many of the above examples, outside consultants, trainers or facilitators provide support to network participants. Sometimes network members who are practiced in a particular approach to conflict resolution train other network members. While outside counsel is not absolutely necessary, network participants can sometimes more effectively pursue their common purpose in the presence of resource people adept at establishing a supportive and productive group atmosphere. Few network members will argue against the value of having available people skilled in helping point out and balance differentials in power, persuasion techniques and public speaking confidence or capability.

12. **What funding and other resources will the network need and where will they come from?**

Think creatively about how to identify, tap and deploy various resource streams. Consider a variety of approaches to funding whether used alone or in combination, including:

FUNDING THROUGH MEMBER CASH CONTRIBUTIONS.
Beyond the expected contributions of commitment
to the common purpose and regular participation,
network members may decide to fund the network
through financial "self-assessment." Self-assessment
means supplying funds from individual organizations
to finance network operations. Such an approach can
provide network members with certainty and a sense
of collective control over the network. Self-assessment
formulas and agreements need to offer budgeting
predictability for members, cover some or all of the
costs of network operations, include mechanisms for
periodic review and foster a sense of equity among
members. Funding self-assessment schemes have a
way of clarifying in a very direct way member
commitment. They also focus member attention and
help members ascribe tangible value to desired
network results.

TOTAL OR PARTIAL SUPPORT THROUGH MEMBER
IN-KIND CONTRIBUTIONS.
In-kind contributions of staff time and expertise,
office space, materials and services, such as postage,
printing, copying and telephones, that would otherwise require raising funds are another form of self-
assessment. Like commitments of cash, in-kind
contributions represent tangible investments by
members in the success of the network. They also
sharpen each contributing member's ownership of
network results.

GRANT SEEKING FOR GENERAL OPERATIONS.
Networks may choose to approach private, corporate
or community foundations for general operating funds
over extended time frames, usually best measured
]in years. The Water Forum received funding largely
allocated by city and county government agencies.
The most likely funders will be those predisposed to
understand the leverage that networked action can
provide to their grant funds. Short-term, start-up
grants can be useful, but networks that launch a long-
term agenda with only short-term funding and no
other means of support risk early collapse and failure.

GRANT SEEKING FOR PROJECT ACTIVITIES.
Networks that achieve early and visible gains may
find themselves sufficiently credible to qualify for
project grants in areas important to accomplishing
the network's purpose and of interest to particular
funders. For example, networks that form action
groups involved in working through compelling issues
related to the network's larger purpose may attract
"project" or "work group" grants that the network
can administer. Budgeting for any project grant
should include line items in the budget to cover a fair
share of staffing and administering the network.

> The most likely
> funders will be
> those predisposed
> to understand
> the leverage that
> networked action
> can provide to their
> grant funds.

Choices about the sources, stability and duration of
network funding cannot be taken lightly. Member-funded
networks will carry with them as many, though perhaps
different, expectations about network accountability as
will externally funded networks. All funders have expec-

tations that the money they commit to an effort will produce tangible, even measurable results. It should come as no surprise to network participants that funders may want to influence grantee agendas, attach explicit or implicit grant performance expectations or enjoy privileged access to network deliberations. Such expectations cannot be pushed aside. They represent a potential source of conflict, which must be confronted squarely in networks. Network members need to anticipate and plan for how they will manage funder expectations before those expectations arise.

Maximum *flexibility* in funding uses should be a network watchword that guides decisions about accepting any funding from any source. Networks should develop a healthy preference for driving their own agenda, even waiting to present the network plan in a relatively advanced state of development to outside funders for needed support. In negotiating start-up or ongoing support, networks should avoid agreeing to funding terms that skew the network agenda away from what members have decided or that run counter in any way to the stated network purpose. Members should explicitly decide whether outside funders meet the requirements for membership. If funders do not qualify, network members always have the option of offering them special status, perhaps as welcome observers and occasional advisors. Networks funded with public tax monies from city, county, special district, state or federal sources may need to comply with legal requirements for transparency and open meetings.

All funders have expectations that the money they commit to an effort will produce tangible, even measurable results.

13. **What other key resources do we need to have in place?**

Other necessary resources to have in place include administrative support to facilitate network management and coordination, outside professional counsel and expertise and, most important, the time and participation of designated member organization representatives.

ADMINISTRATIVE SUPPORT. Administrative support activities and requirements range widely. They may include handling meeting logistics, keeping and maintaining network records, summarizing notes from work group meetings, managing and updating databases or Web sites, printing and distributing reports and materials, answering phone queries or coordinating periodic convenings. Network members may decide to include administrative support personnel as part of the overall network budget. Alternatively, one or more members, as part of an in-kind contribution to the network, may dedicate part- or full-time administrative support to meet network needs.

OUTSIDE PROFESSIONAL EXPERTISE. Depending on what the network intends to accomplish, addressing network priorities may require various sorts of outside professional expertise. Some networks may want to commission independent research to gather facts and provide analysis on topics of concern. Others may want to strengthen themselves in areas where collective member expertise is missing or weak. As discussed

earlier, network members may realize they need
training or skilled counsel in resolving conflicts and
disputes.

TIME AND ENGAGED PARTICIPATION. Member
representatives to the network must allow sufficient
time for the kinds of engagement that lead to new
relationships and advance the network purpose. This
most critical of resources comes with a price – time
away from other activities in their own organization –
and cannot be undervalued. Still, if network participation stands any chance of enabling member groups
to more effectively pursue their common purpose in
ways that better fulfill individual organization missions,
the time spent "in network" should prove worth the
investment.

CHAPTER 4

What to Watch As Your Network Works

As DISCUSSED EARLIER, groups organizing into networks will always encounter difficulties. Organizers can hurt themselves and prospective members by lulling them to believe that, by establishing a network, all problems will disappear. In reality, networks mean greater complexity for inter-organizational relationships. The decision to form the network – and all it entails – needs to be the better trade-off when compared to business as usual.

Even when groups tackle (and overcome) the conflicts that arise in the creation of a network, issues will continue to arise. Members participating in a network will find themselves defaulting to traditional roles with which they feel comfortable and successful in their own organizations. For example, although they may intellectually under-stand and accept that "no one is in charge" in a network, members may cling to a desire to be in charge, especially if that is their role in their individual organization. All members need to be fully aware of this tendency to revert to more comfortable roles, discovering in this awareness new ways of fostering relationships as equal partners with other network members.

Forming the network needs to be the better tradeoff...

Other difficulties may also arise and must not be ignored. They will not go away unless brought out into the open and dealt with in a process understood by, participated in and acceptable to all members. Without an ongoing commitment to clear, open and sustained communication and adoption of a conflict or dispute resolution process, the foundation for an effective network will be shaky at best.

Monitoring Progress and Maintaining Continuity

...maintain a high level of vigilance to preserve good network conditions.

Because a range of both internal and external developments can influence the network for better or worse, maintain a high level of vigilance to preserve good network conditions. Anticipate confronting some of the following issues at various times as the network progresses. The questions in each issue area can help guide a productive periodic review process.

Assessing and Tracking Progress

- What have we tangibly accomplished in fulfilling our purpose as a network that individual member organizations and institutions could not have accomplished alone?
- How have the people served by our network members benefited as a result of changes we have created or influenced through the network's action?
- How have relationships among members of the network changed?

- How have the workings of each member organization changed as a result of participation in the network?

Continuity of Network Purpose

- Has the network's purpose changed?
- If so, is there agreement from everyone and a full understanding of the implications?
- Does the change have an impact on the network's legitimacy?

Operational Continuity

- Has the way the network operates changed?
- What factors have led to the changes and are all members aware of and agreeable to the changes?
- What impact have operational changes had on member participation in all aspects of the network's activities?

Member Participation and Contributions

- To what extent are members participating regularly and substantively?
- To what extent are members contributing resources to the network?
- To what extent has any member's influence or contribution grown disproportionate to that of other members or otherwise altered network equilibrium?
- How have we enforced sanctions for members who do not contribute or honor their commitments?

Membership Changes

- Have we opened participation to new organizations and institutions?
- If so, how well have we oriented new members to the network's purpose, our history, our agreements, our priorities, our methods of managing and resolving conflict, and the results we have achieved?
- Have members left the network? If so, what factors have influenced their decision to leave?
- What do the member departures say about the effectiveness of the network?
- What have we done to reinvigorate member commitment to the network purpose and prevent burnout?

Decision-Making and Conflict Resolution Processes

- To what extent does the full membership have a concrete role in making decisions?
- Has member involvement been consistent?
- What decision-making processes have we found work best for us?
- What additional decision-making skills and training would serve us well?
- How effective have we been at anticipating, surfacing and resolving conflicts?
- When conflicts arise, have we mined them fully for the opportunities they represent to understand one another better and address our common purpose more effectively?
- What additional conflict resolution skills and training would serve us well?

A Few Final Thoughts

A HANDFUL OF KEY CONCEPTS emerge again and again in the preceding discussion about networks that work. They comprise a set of guiding principles that contribute to network longevity and effectiveness and include:

- Focus on shared purpose.
- Start from pre-existing relationships.
- Determine network member tolerance for risk.
- Respect organizational and institutional autonomy.
- Assure up-front commitment from key players.
- Build new types of relationships.
- Emphasize equal partnership.
- Expect – even embrace – conflict, and develop practices for anticipating, surfacing and resolving it.
- Secure needed resources for operation without letting suppliers distort or diffuse the network purpose.

Any attempt to incorporate these principles into the tasks, activities and management of any style of network will give rise to challenges and constraints. Those to remain aware of include:

- Higher stakes and correspondingly higher risks as network ambitions grow.
- The needed investment of time in setting up the network, agreeing on priorities and translating them into action.
- The need to develop new habits of thinking not just organizationally, but also at the network level.
- The importance of distinguishing the basic differences between what it takes to lead and direct an organization well and what it takes to manage and facilitate a network comprised of many autonomous organizations.
- The need to identify and appreciate – beyond substantive network-driven accomplishments – the more intangible results that accrue in the form of new relationships, values and perceptions.
- The unavoidable – and ultimately beneficial – importance of raising, confronting and working through difficult political, cultural and style differences that invariably arise between organizations that choose to work together.

When organizations succeed in joining forces for the greater good, when the shared purpose comes first, the outcomes often can far exceed what any single group can achieve individually.

But of course, keep in mind the potential of a network that works. When organizations succeed in joining forces for the greater good, when the shared purpose comes first, the outcomes often can far exceed what any single group can achieve individually. Indeed, addressing some large-scale public issues requires networked action. When networks work, everyone wins.

We hope this guide has provided you and your organization with useful tools and illustrative case studies as you consider, form and evolve your network. We encourage you to share your thoughts and experiences with us. Your feedback will help ensure that any future editions continue to reflect the most current needs and best practices of the full range of networks. Please forward your comments to *networks@CommunityPartners.org*.

Appendices

North American Alliance for Fair Employment (NAAFE)

The Issue

A wide spectrum of advocacy and activist groups, beginning in 1997, looked for a way to join together to examine the issues and promote the rights of contingent workers. Encouraged by a progressive private foundation, the groups convened a large general assembly and agreed on a network structure.

The groups wanted the network to provide a flow of useful information about contingent work issues, shape both local and national discourse on contingent work, link organizations across divides of geography, structure, program and constituency, and establish groundwork for future funder support of their activities and advocacy. But was it too much to ask?

Cooperative Network Example

The Challenges

In the beginning, bridging so many diverse interests seemed the most challenging: Construction workers and other labor unions, professionals from the high-tech industry, university graduate assistants and undocumented immigrants all held their own, unique perspectives and definitions regarding the same issue. But more significant hurdles would beset the membership and the network itself a few years down the road.

The Network Solution

An 18-month planning process led to the establishment of the North American Alliance for Fair Employment (NAAFE), with the purpose of garnering collective responses from otherwise fragmented groups around the broad issue of contingent work and economic restructuring.

By 2006, NAAFE consisted of 65 organizations from both Canada and the U.S. A volunteer coordinating committee received support from a small "secretariat" staffed by three people. Action groups addressed specific priorities such as the development and advocacy of a "temporary workers' bill of rights," to the operators of agencies placing temporary workers in business settings. Member organizations can point to a number of important accomplishments achieved by the network, not the least of which was an annual (and, later, biannual) general assembly at which members shared with one another both successes and challenges encountered in their individual organizations.

With significantly diminished foundation grant funds now available to NAAFE and no provision in place for member groups to self-finance the network, initial high energy has dissipated. NAAFE has merged under another organization, Massachusetts Global Action (MGA), and MGA staff has refocused NAAFE activities sharply. Two critical issues propelling the realignment: (1) a lack of clarity regarding the authority of staff versus the coordinating committee, a problem with roots in the original network agreement, and (2) the perceived, potential or actual influence of private funders as well as belief on the part of members that funder affiliation might lead to greater individual member grants.

The Successes

Despite its challenges, NAAFE has achieved not just longevity, but a number of concrete, and very positive, results, including:

- Coordination that led to greater focus in New England on rising anti-immigrant movement issues.
- Development of a delegation of 50 people who attended the World Social Forum/Caucus on issues in globalization in January 2006.
- Several key publications widely disseminated in the field.
- Creation of a useful and easily accessible Web site as a resource for members and other groups.

For More Information

Go to *www.fairjobs.org* or *www.massglobalaction.org*.

To access a more in-depth version of this and other related case studies, please visit *www.CommunityPartners.org/ networks*.

The California Partnership

The Issue

After working together on an effort to influence federal policy around jobs and income for poor families, a diverse group of community-based advocacy and service organizations from Los Angeles sought to harness their collective power with a statewide coalition of their own. But how to connect such a large, disparate group?

The Challenges

Initial challenges to creating a network were many. Groups were distinct and disconnected in their work. Their advocacy efforts often overlapped, their messages to legislators were uncoordinated. Spread far and wide across the state, they tended to identify their constituencies quite differently. Even with the network in place, members still occasionally lost sight of their common ties with one another and conflicts arose.

Coordinative Network Example

The Network Solution

A responsive, representative structure. A clearly defined and realistic set of mutual expectations. Fiscal support. Success by The California Partnership on these critical fronts has helped unite dozens of groups as an effective coordinating network in the fight against poverty in California.

Each of the network's five chapters sends one or more representatives to the nine-member Coordinating Committee. The Coordinating Committee's job is to strike the right balance between network priorities and member organization missions. The committee supports member engagement by hearing and shaping various views. Committee representatives then set priorities based on member input, keeping the network's unifying purpose at the forefront. This principle – shared purpose goes first – helped surface and resolve conflicts when friction over priorities arose between some members of the network.

All member organizations sign the network memo of understanding, an agreement outlining member responsibilities to the network. The Center for Community Change serves as the group's fiscal sponsor but does not direct the network.

The Successes

Overall, network members experience a sense of collective strength and accomplish more as a network. Concrete results they point to:

- Greater civic engagement in target communities through the publication and wide distribution of a Voter Guide in six languages.
- A successful tax fairness campaign that included extensive educational activities, outreach, and a tool kit written in English, Spanish and Chinese.

- Legislative testimony and mass mobilization in opposition to proposals in the 2006 California budget process that would have hurt low-income families.
- Unified co-sponsorship and advocacy for SB1639, the "Education Works" bill, which the Governor signed into law.

For More Information

Go to *www.california-partnership.org* where you can find a copy of the agreement executed by The California Partnership's participating members.

To access a more in-depth version of this and other related case studies, please visit *www.CommunityPartners.org/networks*.

The Water Forum

The Issue

Water was and remains the hot-button issue for the Sacramento region of California. By the early 1990s, efforts to manage the water supply while preserving the area's ecological habitat had developed into a contentious, litigious mess. Developers, water purveyors, environmentalists, business owners and executives, agricultural leaders and representatives of various citizen groups all wanted to have a say. But how to bridge those various interests and objectives with the goal of one workable solution?

The Challenges

The issue alone required a solution on a grand scale. One that would not only involve multiple stakeholders and differing interests and agendas, but that would be an ongoing process for decades to come. With long-standing conflicts added to the mix, the issue could have seemed insurmountable. It wasn't just environmentalists suing the water interests, but the water suppliers suing each other. The City and County of Sacramento in 1995 convened the Water Forum in an effort to bring the diverse groups involved closer to a shared way of approaching the problem. They had a long road ahead in addressing the historical feelings of distrust and ill will resulting from highly adversarial relationships.

Collaborative Network Example

The Network Solution

The Water Forum in 2001 became a formalized network, with 40 members signing a historic agreement to work together with common purpose through the year 2030. But this unifying act did not come without years of patience, commitment on the part of all parties involved, significant financial support and, most essential by all accounts, a mediation process ideally suited to the challenges at hand.

All members underwent a common education process prior to entering into a type of mediation called "interest-based negotiation," which focuses on assuring that all voices are heard equally and fairly. Lawsuits were dropped, and the diverse group of stakeholders developed an understanding of one another's concerns and the ability to work together toward a common goal.

A dedicated professional staff provides basic management and a 16-member Coordinating Committee makes policy decisions around dues, budgets and oversight of major work projects. Flexibility, constant communication, inarguable success and a general "pride of ownership" keep the network moving forward productively.

The Successes

The time and commitment members have invested in the Water Forum have paid off for the region. Some of their results include:

- Improved water flow.
- Conservation efforts.
- Expanded groundwater management.
- Habitat programs.
- New water treatment plants.
- Diversion of the American River.
- Replicated networks in other counties.
- Exceptional personal and professional relationships in the water community.

For More Information

Go to *www.waterforum.org* where you can find a copy of the agreement executed by the Water Forum's participating members.

To access a more in-depth version of this and other related case studies, please visit *www.CommunityPartners.org/ networks.*

Position Description

Position Title: Network Manager (alternatively: Network Coordinator, Network Facilitator)

Accountable To: Network Membership through [Network Coordinating Group, or other reporting channel]

Summary of Organizational Role: The Network Manager serves as a key coordinative and facilitative resource to members of the network. The Network Manager helps the network members reach and fulfill the network purpose based on agreements negotiated by members and expressed in the network agreement.

Compensation: [$ amount or "commensurate with experience"].

Duties and Responsibilities:

- Facilitate network member communication, information sharing, interest clarification, and identification and resolution of differences.
- Support directly – or identify and coordinate with outside resources that can support – members with interest negotiation, conflict resolution, meeting management and other needed skills.
- Work with members to identify and prioritize network tasks that will advance shared network purpose.
- Guide, smooth and support efficient interactions among members engaged in network's tasks.

Sample Job Description for a Network Manager

- Facilitate data collection necessary for assessing and evaluating effectiveness of network activities.
- Identify favorable opportunities members can pursue that address and resolve issues critical to network success.
- Locate, help secure and budget financial and other resources needed to support network operations.
- Build the network by helping members identify and bring in new members.
- Facilitate ways to refresh and renew network capabilities, function and focus.

Position Requirements:

- Demonstrated knowledge of and established reputation in the field of [name field or area of interest of the network].
- Demonstrated ability to work productively and masterfully in complex, inter-organizational settings among groups with differing interests.
- Conflict identification, negotiation and resolution skills and experience.
- Outstanding oral and written communications skills.
- Flexibility, adaptability and integrity.

Network Agreement

No network agreement resembles any other agreement. All have unique features particular to the network and its members. Virtually all are voluntary in nature and members decide and enforce explicit standards of accountability. Still, groups developing network agreements, charters, relational contracts or memoranda of understanding should address some or all of the following points in the final written product, depending on the type of network they are developing:

Reasons for Agreement Describes:

- Background rationale for forming the network (perhaps in preamble form).
- Expected duration of the agreement (if intent is to operate for a specific period, otherwise specifies "open-ended" timeframe).

Network Purpose

- Describes the specific shared purpose binding members in common cause.
- Outlines any subsidiary aims that flow from the purpose.

Network Priorities

Anticipates flexibility and change – sometimes on short notice – and requirement for periodic updating. (Priorities will develop and change as the network

Sample Template for a Network Agreement

develops and changes. Member-decided priorities may be listed here but, because they change, often frequently, may be better produced as an addendum or summed up in a periodic communication to members.)

Membership

Describes:

- Membership qualifications for organizations and institutions.
- Process for admitting new members and how they will be oriented.
- Any special forms or categories of membership (observer status, individual experts, advisors, etc.).
- Provisions, reasons, sanctions, processes and procedures for removing members if necessary.

Roles and Commitments of Members

Describes collective member responsibility and expectations, including:

- Commitment to the shared vision.
- Commitment to shared "ownership" of the network and its accomplishments.
- Acknowledgment of potential risks and rewards that accompany participation.
- Commitment to open communication.
- Member commitment to joint decision-making processes.
- Specific monetary and other resources members must commit and contribute.

- General types of activities/tasks expected of members (for meetings, action group participation, etc.).
- Duration of time commitment expected of members to network participation (commitment can be open-ended or – depending on the type of network – it may be desirable to specify a year or more).
- Describes specific authority of a member organization's representative to:
  - Make decisions on behalf of his/her organization.
  - Devote time and commit organizational resources to the network.
- Describes procedure network will follow if/when member organizations decide to send new representatives to the network.

Operational Structure and Procedures

Describes:
- Procedure to develop and periodically review the shared purpose.
- Procedure for developing and periodically reviewing network priorities.
- Procedure to assess and deal with changed internal and external conditions.
- Procedure for tackling and resolving (not avoiding) conflict.
- Procedure for reaching consensus, negotiating, voting, or other processes for moving through deliberation to decision to action.
- Procedures for deciding on and implementing member training (such as in negotiation, listening skills, relationship building techniques).

- Procedure for members to consider and integrate network priorities into their own organizations and institutions.

Role of Staff and Other Needed Support

- Describes staff's facilitative role(s), title, required expertise.
- May anticipate use of consultants, experts, other outside resources.
- Depends on type of network, some of which will not have staff.

Funding and Resources

- Reiterates and summarizes each member's specific expected contributions.
- May contain agreements with or references to separate agreements for resource commitments from key stakeholders.
- Describes process for acquiring resources for network.
- Describes budget for network, if budgeted expenses are anticipated.

Accountability

Describes:
- Member commitment to accountability, to engaging in periodic assessment and evaluation, valuing feedback, etc.
- Frequency of review and evaluation.

- Process for conducting periodic review and evaluation of network effectiveness, accomplishments, structure, functionality, etc. including:
  - Analysis of *internal* network operation.
  - Gathering *external* perceptions from various stakeholders, including network members.
- Actions network will take as a result of the evaluations.

Useful Resources and Web sites

Agranoff, R. (2003). *Leveraging networks: A guide for public managers working across organizations.* Arlington, Virginia: IBM Endowment for The Business of Government.

Agranoff, R. and McGuire, M. (2003). *Collaborative Public Management: New Strategies for Local Governments,* Washington, D.C.: Georgetown University Press.

Connick, S. (2006). *The Sacramento Area Water Forum: A case study.* Institute of Urban & Regional Development, IURD working Paper Series, WP 2006-06. Berkeley: University of California.

Cordero-Guzman, H. R. (May 8, 2001, Revised October 30, 2001). "Interorganizational Networks Among Community-Based Organizations," Unpublished Manuscript, Community Development Research Center, Robert J. Milano Graduate School of Management and Urban Policy, New School University, *hcordero@newschool.edu.*

Crowley, K. (December 2003 – February 2004). "Joined Up Governance: Pushing the Youth Policy Boundaries?" *Today,* Issue 2.

Edwards, S. L. and Stern, R. F. (1998). "Building and Sustaining Community Partnerships for Teen Pregnancy Prevention." A Working Paper. Cornerstone Consulting Group, Inc., *http://aspc.hhs.gov/hsp/teenp/teenpreg.htm.*

Gray, B. (1989). *Collaborating: Finding common ground for multiparty problems*. San Francisco: Jossey-Bass.

Himmelman, Arthur T. (2001). On Coalitions and Transformation of Power Relations: Collaborative Betterment and Collaborative Empowerment. *American Journal of Community Psychology, 29*(2): 277 – 284.

Huxham, C. (Ed) (1996). *Creating collaborative advantage*. London: Sage.

Innes & Booher, "Consensus Building as Role Playing and Bricolage," *Journal of the American Planning Association,* Winter 1999, Vol. 65, No. 1, pages 9-26.

Kamensky, John M. & Thomas Burlin (eds.) (2004). *Collaboration: Using Networks and Partnerships.* Rowman & Littlefield Publishers, Inc., New York.

Kickert, Walter, Erik-Hans Klijn & Joop F.M. Koppenjan (1997). *Managing Complex Networks.* Sage Publications, London.

Koppenjan, J., & Klijn, E-H. (2004). *Managing uncertainties in networks*. London: Routledge.

Lipnack, J., & Stamps, J. (1994). *The age of the network*. New York: Wiley.

Mandell, M.P (Ed.) (2001). Getting results through collaboration: networks and network structures for public policy and management. Westport: Quorum Books.